I0115954

Abnormal Psychology

Editor

Juliann Moen

Scribbles

Year of Publication 2018

ISBN : 9789352979608

Book Published by

Scribbles

(An Imprint of Alpha Editions)

email - alphaedis@gmail.com

Produced by: PediaPress GmbH
Limburg an der Lahn
Germany
http://pediapress.com/

Contents

History of mental disorders

Historical conceptions of abnormal behavior

For thousands of years, humans have tried to explain and control problematic behavior. But our efforts always derive from theories or models of behavior popular at the time, and the purpose is to explain 'why someone is like that'. Three major models, namely, supernatural model, biological model and psychological model.

Supernatural tradition

For much of our recorded history, deviant behavior has been considered a reflection of the battle between good and evil. When confronted with unexplainable, irrational behavior and by suffering and upheaval, people have perceived evil. In fact, in the Great Persian Empire from 900 to 600 B.C., all physical and mental disorders were considered the work of the devil.

Biological tradition

Physical causes of mental disorders have been sought in history. Important to this tradition are a man, Hippocrates; a disease, syphilis; and the early consequences of believing that psychological disorders are biologically caused.

Psychological tradition

This was a precursor to modern psychosocial treatment approaches to the causation of psychopathology, with the focus on psychological, social and cultural factors. Well known philosophers like Aristotle, Plato, etc., wrote about the importance of fantasies, dreams, cognitions, and thus anticipated, to some extent, later developments in psychoanalytic thought and cognitive science. They also advocated humane and responsible care for individuals with psychological disturbances.

Ancient period

Mesopotamia

Mental illnesses were well known in ancient Mesopotamia, where diseases and mental disorders were believed to be caused by specific deities. Because hands symbolized control over a person, mental illnesses were known as "hands" of certain deities. One psychological illness was known as *Qāt Ištar*, meaning "Hand of Ishtar". Others were known as "Hand of Shamash", "Hand of the Ghost", and "Hand of the God". Descriptions of these illnesses, however, are so vague that it is usually impossible to determine which illnesses they correspond to in modern terminology. Mesopotamian doctors kept detailed record of their patients' hallucinations and assigned spiritual meanings to them. A patient who hallucinated that he was seeing a dog was predicted to die; whereas, if he saw a gazelle, he would recover. The royal family of Elam was notorious for its members frequently suffering from insanity. Erectile dysfunction was recognized as being rooted in psychological problems.

Egypt

Limited notes in an ancient Egyptian document known as the Ebers papyrus appear to describe the affected states of concentration, attention, and emotional distress in the heart or mind. Some of these were interpreted later, and renamed as hysteria and melancholy. Somatic treatments included applying bodily fluids while reciting magical spells. Hallucinogens may have been used as a part of the healing rituals. Religious temples may have been used as therapeutic retreats, possibly for the induction of receptive states to facilitate sleep and the interpretation of dreams.

India

Ancient Hindu scriptures-Ramayana and Mahabharata-contain fictional descriptions of depression and anxiety. Mental disorders were generally thought to reflect abstract metaphysical entities, supernatural agents, sorcery and witchcraft. The Charaka Samhita from circa 600 BC, which is a part of the Hindu Ayurveda ("knowledge of life"), saw ill health as resulting from an imbalance among the three body fluids or forces called Tri-Dosha. These also affected the personality types among people. Suggested causes included inappropriate diet, disrespect towards the gods, teachers or others, mental shock due to excessive fear or joy, and faulty bodily activity. Treatments included the use of herbs and ointments, charms and prayers, and moral or emotional persuasion.

China

The earliest known record of mental illness in ancient China dates back to 1100 B.C. Mental disorders were treated mainly under Traditional Chinese Medicine using herbs, acupuncture or "emotional therapy". The Inner Canon of the Yellow Emperor described symptoms, mechanisms and therapies for mental illness, emphasizing connections between bodily organs and emotions. The ancient Chinese believed that demonic possession played a role in mental illness during this time period. They felt that areas of emotional outbursts such as funeral homes could open up the Wei Chi and allow entities to possess an individual. Trauma was also considered to be something that caused high levels of emotion. Thus, trauma is a possible catalyst for mental illness, due to its ability to allow the Wei Chi open to possession. This explains why the ancient Chinese believed that a mental illness was in reality a demonic possession. According to Chinese thought, five stages or elements comprised the conditions of imbalance between Yin and yang. Mental illness, according to the Chinese perspective is thus considered as an imbalance of the yin and yang because optimum health arises from balance with nature.

China was one of the earliest developed civilizations in which medicine and attention to mental disorders were introduced (Soong, 2006)As in the West, Chinese views of mental disorders regressed to a belief in supernatural forces as causal agents. From the later part of the second century through the early part of the ninth century, ghosts and devils were implicated in "ghostevil" insanity, which presumably resulted from possession by evil spirits. The "Dark Ages" in China, however, were neither so severe (in terms of the treatment of mental patients) nor as long-lasting as in the West. A return to biological, somatic (bodily) views and an emphasis on psychosocial factors occurred in the centuries that followed. Over the past 50 years, China has been experiencing a broadening of ideas in mental health services and has been incorporating many ideas from Western psychiatry (Zhang & Lu, 2006)

Greece and Rome

In ancient Greece and Rome, madness was associated stereotypically with aimless wandering and violence. However, Socrates considered positive aspects including prophesying (a 'manic art'); mystical initiations and rituals; poetic inspiration; and the madness of lovers. Now often seen as the very epitome of rational thought and as the founder of philosophy, Socrates freely admitted to experiencing what are now called "command hallucinations" (then called his 'daemon'). Pythagoras also heard voices. Hippocrates (470–ca. 360 BC) classified mental disorders, including paranoia, epilepsy, mania and melancholia.

Through long contact with Greek culture, and their eventual conquest of Greece, the Romans absorbed many Greek (and other) ideas on medicine.

The humoral theory fell out of favor in some quarters. The Greek physician Asclepiades (ca. 124–40 BC), who practiced in Rome, discarded it and advocated humane treatments, and had insane persons freed from confinement and treated them with natural therapy, such as diet and massages. Arateus (ca. AD 30–90) argued that it is hard to pinpoint from where a mental illness comes. However, Galen (AD 129–ca. 200), practicing in Greece and Rome, revived humoral theory. Galen, however, adopted a single symptom approach rather than broad diagnostic categories, for example studying separate states of sadness, excitement, confusion and memory loss.

Playwrights such as Homer, Sophocles and Euripides described madmen driven insane by the gods, imbalanced humors or circumstances. As well as the triad (of which mania was often used as an overarching term for insanity) there were a variable and overlapping range of terms for such things as delusion, eccentricity, frenzy, and lunacy. Physician Celsus argued that insanity is really present when a continuous dementia begins due to the mind being at the mercy of imaginings. He suggested that people must heal their own souls through philosophy and personal strength. He described common practices of dietetics, bloodletting, drugs, talking therapy, incubation in temples, exorcism, incantations and amulets, as well as restraints and "tortures" to restore rationality, including starvation, being terrified suddenly, agitation of the spirit, and stoning and beating. Most, however, did not receive medical treatment but stayed with family or wandered the streets, vulnerable to assault and derision. Accounts of delusions from the time included people who thought themselves to be famous actors or speakers, animals, inanimate objects, or one of the gods. Some were arrested for political reasons, such as Jesus ben Ananias who was eventually released as a madman after showing no concern for his own fate during torture.

Israel and the Hebrew diaspora

Passages of the Hebrew Bible/Old Testament have been interpreted as describing mood disorders in figures such as Job, King Saul and in the Psalms of David. In the Book of Daniel, King Nebuchadnezzar is described as temporarily losing his sanity. Mental disorder was not a problem like any other, caused by one of the gods, but rather caused by problems in the relationship between the individual and God.Wikipedia:Citation needed They believed that abnormal behavior was the result of possessions that represented the wrath and punishment from God. This punishment was seen as a withdrawal of God's protection and the abandonment of the individual to evil forces.

Middle ages

Persia, Arabia and the Muslim empire

Persian and Arabic scholars were heavily involved in translating, analyzing and synthesizing Greek texts and concepts. As the Muslim world expanded, Greek concepts were integrated with religious thought and over time, new ideas and concepts were developed. Arab texts from this period contain discussions of melancholia, mania, hallucinations, delusions, and other mental disorders. Mental disorder was generally connected to loss of reason, and writings covered links between the brain and disorders, and spiritual/mystical meaning of disorders. wrote about fear and anxiety, anger and aggression, sadness and depression, and obsessions.

Authors who wrote on mental disorders and/or proposed treatments during this period include Al-Balkhi, Al-Razi, Al-Farabi, Ibn-Sina, Al-Majusi Abu al-Qasim al-Zahrawi, Averroes, and Unhammad.

Some thought mental disorder could be caused by possession by a djinn (genie), which could be either good or demon-like. There were sometimes beatings to exorcise the djin, or alternatively over-zealous attempts at cures. Islamic views often merged with local traditions. In Morocco the traditional Berber people were animists and the concept of sorcery was integral to the understanding of mental disorder; it was mixed with the Islamic concepts of djin and often treated by religious scholars combining the roles of holy man, sage, seer and sorcerer.

The first bimaristan was founded in Baghdad in the 9th century, and several others of increasing complexity were created throughout the Arab world in the following centuries. Some of the bimaristans contained wards dedicated to the care of mentally ill patients,[1] most of whom suffered from debilitating illnesses or exhibited violence.[2] In the centuries to come, the Muslim world would eventually serve as a critical way station of knowledge for Renaissance Europe, through the Latin translations of many scientific Islamic texts. Ibn-Sina's (Avicenna's) Canon of Medicine became the standard of medical science in Europe for centuries, together with works of Hippocrates and Galen.

Christian Europe

Conceptions of madness in the Middle Ages in Europe were a mixture of the divine, diabolical, magical and transcendental. Theories of the four humors (black bile, yellow bile, phlegm, and blood) were applied, sometimes separately (a matter of "physic") and sometimes combined with theories of evil spirits (a matter of "faith"). Arnaldus de Villanova (1235–1313) combined "evil spirit" and Galen-oriented "four humours" theories and promoted trephining as a cure to let demons and excess humours escape. Other bodily remedies in general use included purges, bloodletting and whipping. Madness was often seen as a moral issue, either a punishment for sin or a test of faith and character. Christian theology endorsed various therapies, including fasting and prayer for those estranged from God and exorcism of those possessed by the devil. Thus, although mental disorder was often thought to be due to sin, other more mundane causes were also explored, including intemperate diet and alcohol, overwork, and grief. The Franciscan monk Bartholomeus Anglicus (ca. 1203 – 1272) described a condition which resembles depression in his encyclopedia, *De Proprietatibis Rerum*, and he suggested that music would help. A semi-official tract called the Praerogativa regis distinguished between the "natural born idiot" and the "lunatic". The latter term was applied to those with periods of mental disorder; deriving from either Roman mythology describing people "moonstruck" by the goddess Luna or theories of an influence of the moon.

Episodes of mass dancing mania are reported from the Middle Ages, "which gave to the individuals affected all the appearance of insanity". This was one kind of mass delusion or mass hysteria/panic that has occurred around the world through the millennia.

The care of lunatics was primarily the responsibility of the family. In England, if the family were unable or unwilling, an assessment was made by crown representatives in consultation with a local jury and all interested parties, including the subject himself or herself. The process was confined to those with real estate or personal estate, but it encompassed poor as well as rich and took into account psychological and social issues. Most of those considered lunatics at the time probably had more support and involvement from the community than people diagnosed with mental disorders today. As in other eras, visions were generally interpreted as meaningful spiritual and visionary insights; some may have been causally related to mental disorders, but since hallucinations were culturally supported they may not have had the same connections as today.

Modern period

16th to 18th centuries

Some mentally disturbed people may have been victims of the witch-hunts that spread in waves in early modern Europe. However, those judged insane were increasingly admitted to local workhouses, poorhouses and jails (particularly the "pauper insane") or sometimes to the new private madhouses. Restraints and forcible confinement were used for those thought dangerously disturbed or potentially violent to themselves, others or property. The latter likely grew out of lodging arrangements for single individuals (who, in workhouses, were considered disruptive or ungovernable) then there were a few catering each for only a handful of people, then they gradually expanded (e.g. 16 in London in 1774, and 40 by 1819). By the mid-19th century there would be 100 to 500 inmates in each. The development of this network of madhouses has been linked to new capitalist social relations and a service economy, that meant families were no longer able or willing to look after disturbed relatives.

Madness was commonly depicted in literary works, such as the plays of Shakespeare.

By the end of the 17th century and into the Enlightenment, madness was increasingly seen as an organic physical phenomenon, no longer involving the soul or moral responsibility. The mentally ill were typically viewed as insensitive wild animals. Harsh treatment and restraint in chains was seen as therapeutic, helping suppress the animal passions. There was sometimes a focus on the management of the environment of madhouses, from diet to exercise regimes to number of visitors. Severe somatic treatments were used, similar to those in medieval times. Madhouse owners sometimes boasted of their ability with the whip. Treatment in the few public asylums was also barbaric, often secondary to prisons. The most notorious was Bedlam where at one time spectators could pay a penny to watch the inmates as a form of entertainment.

Concepts based in humoral theory gradually gave way to metaphors and terminology from mechanics and other developing physical sciences. Complex new schemes were developed for the classification of mental disorders, influenced by emerging systems for the biological classification of organisms and medical classification of diseases.

The term "crazy" (from Middle English meaning cracked) and insane (from Latin insanus meaning unhealthy) came to mean mental disorder in this period. The term "lunacy", long used to refer to periodic disturbance or epilepsy, came to be synonymous with insanity. "Madness", long in use in root form since at least the early centuries AD, and originally meaning crippled, hurt or foolish, came to mean loss of reason or self-restraint. "Psychosis", from Greek "principle of life/animation", had varied usage referring to a condition of the mind/soul. "Nervous", from an Indo-European root meaning to wind or twist, meant muscle or vigor, was adopted by physiologists to refer to the body's electrochemical signalling process (thus called the nervous system), and was then used to refer to nervous disorders and neurosis. "Obsession", from a Latin root meaning to sit on or sit against, originally meant to besiege or be possessed by an evil spirit, came to mean a fixed idea that could decompose the mind.

With the rise of madhouses and the professionalization and specialization of medicine, there was considerable incentive for medical doctors to become involved. In the 18th century, they began to stake a claim to a monopoly over madhouses and treatments. Madhouses could be a lucrative business, and many made a fortune from them. There were some bourgeois ex-patient reformers who opposed the often brutal regimes, blaming both the madhouse owners and the medics, who in turn resisted the reforms.

Towards the end of the 18th century, a moral treatment movement developed, that implemented more humane, psychosocial and personalized approaches. Notable figures included the medic Vincenzo Chiarugi in Italy under Enlightenment leadership; the ex-patient superintendent Pussin and the psychologically inclined medic Philippe Pinel in revolutionary France; the Quakers in England, led by businessman William Tuke; and later, in the United States, campaigner Dorothea Dix.

19th century

The 19th century, in the context of industrialization and population growth, saw a massive expansion of the number and size of insane asylums in every Western country, a process called "the great confinement" or the "asylum era". Laws were introduced to compel authorities to deal with those judged insane by family members and hospital superintendents. Although originally based on the concepts and structures of moral treatment, they became large impersonal institutions overburdened with large numbers of people with a complex mix of mental and social-economic problems. The success of moral treatment had cast doubt on the approach of medics, and many had opposed it, but by the mid-19th century many became advocates of it but argued that the mad also often had physical/organic problems, so that both approaches were necessary. This argument has been described as an important step in the profession's eventual success in securing a monopoly on the treatment of lunacy. However, it is well documented that very little therapeutic activity occurred in the new asylum system, that medics were little more than administrators who seldom attended to patients, and then mainly for other physical problems.

Clear descriptions of some syndromes, such as the condition that would later be termed schizophrenia, have been identified as relatively rare prior to the 19th century,[3] although interpretations of the evidence and its implications are inconsistent.

Numerous different classification schemes and diagnostic terms were developed by different authorities, taking an increasingly anatomical-clinical descriptive approach. The term "psychiatry" was coined as the medical specialty became more academically established. Asylum superintendents, later to be psychiatrists, were generally called "alienists" because they were thought to deal with people alienated from society; they adopted largely isolated and managerial roles in the asylums while milder "neurotic" conditions were dealt with by neurologists and general physicians, although there was overlap for conditions such as neurasthenia.

In the United States it was proposed that black slaves who tried to escape were suffering from a mental disorder termed drapetomania. It was then argued in scientific journals that mental disorders were rare under conditions of slavery but became more common following emancipation, and later that mental illness in African Americans was due to evolutionary factors or various negative characteristics, and that they were not suitable for therapeutic intervention.

By the 1870s in North America, officials who ran Lunatic Asylums renamed them Insane Asylums. By the late century, the term "asylum" had lost its original meaning as a place of refuge, retreat or safety, and was associated with abuses that had been widely publicized in the media, including by ex-patient organization the Alleged Lunatics' Friend Society and ex-patients like Elizabeth Packard.

The relative proportion of the public officially diagnosed with mental disorders was increasing, however. This has been linked to various factors, including possibly humanitarian concern; incentives for professional status/money; a lowered tolerance of communities for unusual behavior due to the existence of asylums to place them in (this affected the poor the most); and the strain placed on families by industrialization.

20th century

The turn of the 20th century saw the development of psychoanalysis, which came to the fore later. Kraepelin's classification gained popularity, including the separation of mood disorders from what would later be termed schizophrenia.Wikipedia:Citing sources

Asylum superintendents sought to improve the image and medical status of their profession. Asylum "inmates" were increasingly referred to as "patients" and asylums renamed as hospitals. Referring to people as having a "mental illness" dates from this period in the early 20th century.

In the United States, a "mental hygiene" movement, originally defined in the 19th century, gained momentum and aimed to "prevent the disease of insanity" through public health methods and clinics. The term mental health became more popular, however. Clinical psychology and social work developed as professions alongside psychiatry. Theories of eugenics led to compulsory sterilization movements in many countries around the world for several decades, often encompassing patients in public mental institutions. World War I saw a massive increase of conditions that came to be termed "shell shock".

In Nazi Germany, the institutionalized mentally ill were among the earliest targets of sterilization campaigns and covert "euthanasia" programs. It has been estimated that over 200,000 individuals with mental disorders of all kinds were put to death, although their mass murder has received relatively little historical attention. Despite not being formally ordered to take part, psychiatrists and psychiatric institutions were at the center of justifying, planning and carrying out the atrocities at every stage, and "constituted the connection" to the later annihilation of Jews and other "undesirables" such as homosexuals in the Holocaust.

In other areas of the world, funding was often cut for asylums, especially during periods of economic decline, and during wartime in particular many patients starved to death. Soldiers received increased psychiatric attention, and World War II saw the development in the US of a new psychiatric manual for categorizing mental disorders, which along with existing systems for collecting census and hospital statistics led to the first Diagnostic and Statistical Manual of Mental Disorders (DSM). The International Classification of Diseases (ICD) followed suit with a section on mental disorders.

Previously restricted to the treatment of severely disturbed people in asylums, psychiatrists cultivated clients with a broader range of problems, and between 1917 and 1970 the number practicing outside institutions swelled from 8 percent to 66 percent. The term stress, having emerged from endocrinology work in the 1930s, was popularized with an increasingly broad biopsychosocial meaning, and was increasingly linked to mental disorders. "Outpatient commitment" laws were gradually expanded or introduced in some countries.

Lobotomies, Insulin shock therapy, Electro convulsive therapy, and the "neuroleptic" chlorpromazine came into use mid-century.

An antipsychiatry movement came to the fore in the 1960s. Deinstitutionalization gradually occurred in the West, with isolated psychiatric hospitals being closed down in favor of community mental health services. However, inadequate services and continued social exclusion often led to many being homeless or in prison. A consumer/survivor movement gained momentum.

Other kinds of psychiatric medication gradually came into use, such as "psychic energizers" and lithium. Benzodiazepines gained widespread use in the 1970s for anxiety and depression, until dependency problems curtailed their popularity. Advances in neuroscience and genetics led to new research agendas. Cognitive behavioral therapy was developed. Through the 1990s, new SSRI antidepressants became some of the most widely prescribed drugs in the world.

The DSM and then ICD adopted new criteria-based classification, representing a return to a Kraepelin-like descriptive system. The number of "official" diagnoses saw a large expansion, although homosexuality was gradually downgraded and dropped in the face of human rights protests. Different regions sometimes developed alternatives such as the Chinese Classification of Mental Disorders or Latin American Guide for Psychiatric Diagnosis.

21st century

USA

DSM-IV and previous versions of the *Diagnostic and Statistical Manual of Mental Disorders* presented extremely high comorbidity, diagnostic heterogeneity of the categories, unclear boundaries, that have been interpreted as intrinsic anomalies of the criterial, neopositivistic approach leading the system to a state of scientific crisis. Accordingly, a radical rethinking of the concept of mental disorder and the need of a radical scientific revolution in psychiatric taxonomy was proposed.

In 2013, the American Psychiatric Association published the *DSM–5* after more than 10 years of research.

History of mental health treatment
4

Prehistory

There is archealogical evidence for the use of trepanation in around 6500 BC.

Antiquity

Hippocrates mentions the practice of bloodletting in the fifth century BC.

Medieval era

In 1377, lunatics were moved from Stone House to Bethlem, one of the first psychiatric institutions.

19th Century

The "oldest forensic secure hospital in Europe" was opened in 1850 after Sir Thomas Freemantle introduced the bill that was to establish a Central Criminal Lunatic Asylum in Ireland in May 19th 1845.

20th Century

In early 20th century, lobotomy was introduced till the mid-1950s.

In 1927 insulin coma therapy was introduced and used till 1960. Physicians deliberately put the patient into a low blood sugar coma because they thought that large fluctuations in insulin levels could alter the function of the brain. Risks included prolonged coma. Electroconvulsive Therapy (ECT) was later adopted as a substitution to this.

Further reading

- Millon, Theodore (2004). *Masters of the Mind: Exploring the Story of Mental Illness from Ancient Times to the New Millennium*[5]. Hoboken, NJ: Wiley. ISBN 978-0-471-46985-8. OCLC 54460256[6] – via Google Books.<templatestyles src="Module:Citation/CS1/styles.css"></templatestyles>
- Kent, Deborah (2003). *Snake Pits, Talking Cures & Magic Bullets: A History of Mental Illness*[7]. Brookfield, CT: Twenty-First Century Books. ISBN 978-0-7613-2704-2. OCLC 50253057[8] – via Google Books.<templatestyles src="Module:Citation/CS1/styles.css"></templatestyles>
- Scull, Andrew (1989). *Social Order/Mental Disorder: Anglo-American Psychiatry in Historical Perspective*[9]. Medicine and society. **3**. Berkeley: University of California Press. ISBN 978-0-520-06406-5. OCLC 17982761[10] – via California Digital Library.<templatestyles src="Module:Citation/CS1/styles.css"></templatestyles> ∂
- Foucault, Michel (1961). *Histoire de la folie à l'âge classique* [*Madness and Civilization*]. Collection Tel (in French). **9**. Gallimard. ISBN 978-2-07-029582-1. OCLC 45404661[11].<templatestyles src="Module:Citation/CS1/styles.css"></templatestyles>
- Quétel, Claude (2009). *Histoire de la folie : De l'Antiquité à nos jours* (in French). Paris: Editions Tallandier, Texto. ISBN 978-2-84734-927-6. OCLC 818987861[12].<templatestyles src="Module:Citation/CS1/styles.css"></templatestyles>
- Hurd, Henry M.; Drewry, William F.; Dewey, Richard; Pilgrim, Charles W.; Blumer, G. Adler; Burgess, T.J.W. (1916). Hurd, Henry Mills, ed. *The Institutional Care of the Insane in the United States and Canada*[13]. **1**. Baltimore, MD: Johns Hopkins Press – via Google Books.<templatestyles src="Module:Citation/CS1/styles.css"></templatestyles> ∂

Abnormal psychology

Part of a series on
Psychology
Ψ
• **Outline**   • **History**   • **Subfields**
• Ψ **Psychology portal**
• $\underline{v}$ • $\underline{t}$ • $\underline{e}$[14]

Abnormal psychology is the branch of psychology that studies unusual patterns of behavior, emotion and thought, which may or may not be understood as precipitating a mental disorder. Although many behaviors could be considered as abnormal, this branch of psychology generally deals with behavior in a clinical context.[15] There is a long history of attempts to understand and control behavior deemed to be aberrant or deviant (statistically, functionally, morally or in some other sense), and there is often cultural variation in the approach taken. The field of abnormal psychology identifies multiple causes for different conditions, employing diverse theories from the general field of psychology and elsewhere, and much still hinges on what exactly is meant by "abnormal". There has traditionally been a divide between psychological and biological explanations, reflecting a philosophical dualism in regard to the mind-body problem. There have also been different approaches in trying to classify mental disorders. Abnormal includes three different categories; they are subnormal, supernormal and paranormal.

The science of abnormal psychology studies two types of behaviors: adaptive and maladaptive behaviors. Behaviors that are maladaptive suggest that some problem(s) exist, and can also imply that the individual is vulnerable and cannot cope with environmental stress, which is leading them to have problems functioning in daily life in their emotions, mental thinking, physical actions and talks. Behaviors that are adaptive are ones that are well-suited to the nature of people, their lifestyles and surroundings, and to the people that they communicate with, allowing them to understand each other. Clinical psychology is the applied field of psychology that seeks to assess, understand and treat psychological conditions in clinical practice. The theoretical field known as 'abnormal psychology' may form a backdrop to such work, but clinical psychologists in the current field are unlikely to use the term 'abnormal' in reference to their practice. Psychopathology is a similar term to abnormal psychology but has more of an implication of an underlying pathology (disease process), and as such is a term more commonly used in the medical specialty known as psychiatry.

History

Supernatural traditions

Throughout time, societies have proposed several explanations of abnormal behavior within human beings. Beginning in some hunter-gatherer societies, animists have believed that people demonstrating abnormal behavior are possessed by malevolent spirits. This idea has been associated with trepanation, the practice of cutting a hole into the individual's skull in order to release the malevolent spirits.[16] Although it has been difficult to define abnormal psychology, one definition includes characteristics such as statistical infrequency.

A more formalized response to spiritual beliefs about abnormality is the practice of exorcism. Performed by religious authorities, exorcism is thought of as another way to release evil spirits who cause pathological behavior within the person. In some instances, individuals exhibiting unusual thoughts or behaviors have been exiled from society or worse. Perceived witchcraft, for example, has been punished by death. Two Catholic Inquisitors wrote the *Malleus Maleficarum* (Latin for "The Hammer Against Witches"), that was used by many Inquisitors and witch-hunters. It contained an early taxonomy of perceived deviant behavior and proposed guidelines for prosecuting deviant individuals.

Asylums

The act of placing mentally ill individuals in a separate facility known as an asylum dates to 1547, when King Henry VIII of England established the St. Mary of Bethlehem asylum in London. This hospital, nicknamed Bedlam, was famous for its deplorable conditions.[17] Asylums remained popular throughout the Middle Ages and the Renaissance era. These early asylums were often in miserable conditions. Patients were seen as a "burden" to society and locked away and treated almost as beasts to be dealt with rather than patients needing treatment. However, many of the patients received helpful medical treatment. There was scientific curiosity into abnormal behavior although it was rarely investigated in the early asylums. Inmates in these early asylums were often put on display for profit as they were viewed as less than human. The early asylums were basically modifications of the existing criminal institutions.

In the late 18th century the idea of humanitarian treatment for the patients gained much favor due to the work of Philippe Pinel in France. He pushed for the idea that the patients should be treated with kindness and not the cruelty inflicted on them as if they were animals or criminals. His experimental ideas such as removing the chains from the patients were met with reluctance. The experiments in kindness proved to be a great success, which helped to bring about a reform in the way mental institutions would be run..

Institutionalization would continue to improve throughout the 19th and 20th century due to work of many humanitarians such as Dorethea Dix, and the mental hygiene movement which promoted the physical well-being of the mental patients. "Dix more than any other figure in the nineteenth century, made people in America and virtually all of Europe aware that the insane were being subjected to incredible abuses."[18] Through this movement millions of dollars were raised to build new institutions to house the mentally ill. Mental hospitals began to grow substantially in numbers during the 20th century as care for the mentally ill increased in them.

By 1939 there were over 400,000 patients in state mental hospitals in the USA. Hospital stays were normally quite long for the patients, with some individuals being treated for many years. These hospitals while better than the asylums of the past were still lacking in the means of effective treatment for the patients, and even though the reform movement had occurred; patients were often still met with cruel and inhumane treatment.

Things began to change in the year 1946 when Mary Jane Ward published the influential book titled "The Snake Pit" which was made into a popular movie of the same name. The book called attention to the conditions which mental patients faced and helped to spark concern in the general public to create more humane mental health care in these overcrowded hospitals.

In this same year the National Institute of Mental Health was also created which provided support for the training of hospital employees and research into the conditions which afflicted the patients. During this period the Hill-Burton Acts was also passed which was a program that funded mental health hospitals. Along with the Community Health Services Act of 1963, the Hill-Burton Acts helped with the creation of outpatient psychiatric clinics, inpatient general hospitals, and rehabilitation and community consultation centers.

Deinstitutionalisation

In the late twentieth century however, a large number of mental hospitals were closed due to lack of funding and overpopulation. In England for example only 14 of the 130 psychiatric institutions that had been created in the early 20th century remained open at the start of the 21st century. In 1963, President John Kennedy launched the community health movement in the United States as a "bold new approach" to mental health care, aimed at coordinating mental health services for citizens in mental health centers. In the span of 40 years, the United States was able to see an about 90 percent drop in the number of patients in Psychiatric hospitals.[19]

This trend was not only in the England and the United States but worldwide with countries like Australia having too many mentally ill patients and not enough treatment facilities. Recent studies have found that the prevalence of mental illness has not decreased significantly in the past 10 years, and has in fact increased in frequency regarding specific conditions such as anxiety and mood disorders.

This led to a large number of the patients being released while not being fully cured of the disorder they were hospitalized for. This became known as the phenomenon of deinstitutionalization. This movement had noble goals of treating the individuals outside of the isolated mental hospital by placing them into communities and support systems. Another goal of this movement was to avoid the potential negative adaptations that can come with long term hospital confinements. Many professionals for example were concerned that patients would find permanent refuge in mental hospitals which would take them up when the demands of everyday life were too difficult. However, the patients moved to the community living have not fared well typically, as they often speak of how they feel "abandoned" by the doctors who used to treat them. It also has had the unfortunate effect of placing many of the patients in homelessness. Many safe havens for the deinstitutionalized mentally ill have been created, but it is nevertheless estimated that around 26.2% of people who are currently homeless have some form of a mental illness. The placing of these individuals in homelessness is of major concern to their wellbeing as the added stress of living on the streets is not beneficial for the individual to recover from the particular disorder with which they are afflicted. In fact while some of the homeless who are able to find some temporary relief in the form of shelters, many of the homeless with a mental illness "lack safe and decent shelter".[20]

Explaining abnormal behaviour

People have tried to explain and control abnormal behavior for thousands of years. Historically, there have been three main approaches to abnormal behavior: the supernatural, biological, and psychological traditions.[21] Abnormal psychology revolves around two major paradigms for explaining mental disorders, the *psychological* paradigm and the *biological* paradigm. The psychological paradigm focuses more on the humanistic, cognitive and behavioral causes and effects of psychopathology. The biological paradigm includes the theories that focus more on physical factors, such as genetics and neurochemistry.

Supernatural explanations

In the first supernatural tradition, also called the demonological method, abnormal behaviors are attributed to agents outside human bodies. According to this model, abnormal behaviors are caused by demons, spirits, or the influences of moon, planets, and stars. During the Stone Age, trepanning was performed on those who had mental illness to literally cut the evil spirits out of the victim's head. Conversely, Ancient Chinese, Ancient Egyptians, and Hebrews, believed that these were evil demons or spirits and advocated exorcism. By the time of the Greeks and Romans, mental illnesses were thought to be caused by an imbalance of the four humors, leading to draining of fluids from the brain. During the Medieval period, many Europeans believed that the power of witches, demons, and spirits caused abnormal behaviors. People with psychological disorders were thought to be possessed by evil spirits that had to be exercised through religious rituals. If exorcism failed, some authorities advocated steps such as confinement, beating, and other types of torture to make the body uninhabitable by witches, demons, and spirits. The belief that witches, demons, and spirits are responsible for the abnormal behavior continued into the 15th century.[22] Swiss alchemist, astrologer, and physician Paracelsus (1493–1541), on the other hand, rejected the idea that abnormal behaviors were caused by witches, demons, and spirits and suggested that people's mind and behaviors were influenced by the movements of the moon and stars.[23]

This tradition is still alive today. Some people, especially in the developing countries and some followers of religious sects in the developed countries, continue to believe that supernatural powers influence human behaviors. In Western academia, the supernatural tradition has been largely replaced by the biological and psychological traditions.[24]

Biological explanations

In the biological tradition, psychological disorders are attributed to biological causes and in the psychological tradition, disorders are attributed to faulty psychological development and to social context. The medical or biological perspective holds the belief that most or all abnormal behavior can be attributed to a medical factor; assuming all psychological disorders are diseases.

The Greek physician Hippocrates, who is considered to be the father of Western medicine, played a major role in the biological tradition. Hippocrates and his associates wrote the Hippocratic Corpus between 450 and 350 BC, in which they suggested that abnormal behaviors can be treated like any other disease. Hippocrates viewed the brain as the seat of consciousness, emotion, intelligence, and wisdom and believed that disorders involving these functions would logically be located in the brain.

These ideas of Hippocrates and his associates were later adopted by Galen, the Roman physician. Galen extended these ideas and developed a strong and influential school of thought within the biological tradition that extended well into the 18th century.

Medical: Kendra Cherry states: "The medical approach to abnormal psychology focuses on the biological causes on mental illness. This perspective emphasizes understanding the underlying cause of disorders, which might include genetic inheritance, related physical disorders, infections and chemical imbalances. Medical treatments are often pharmacological in nature, although medication is often used in conjunction with some other type of psychotherapy."

Psychological explanations

Underdeveloped Superego

According to Sigmund Freud's structural model, the Id, Ego and Superego are three theoretical constructs that defines the way an individual interacts with the external world as well as responding to internal forces. The Id represents the instinctual drives of an individual that remain unconscious; the superego represents a person's conscience and their internalization of societal norms and morality; and finally the ego serves to realistically integrate the drives of the id with the prohibitions of the super-ego. Lack of development in the Superego, or an incoherently developed Superego within an individual, will result in thoughts and actions that are irrational and abnormal, contrary to the norms and beliefs of society.

Irrational beliefs

Irrational beliefs that are driven by unconscious fears, can result in abnormal behavior. Rational emotive therapy helps to drive irrational and maladaptive beliefs out of one's mind.

Sociocultural influences

The term sociocultural refers to the various circles of influence on the individual ranging from close friends and family to the institutions and policies of a country or the world as a whole. Discriminations, whether based on social class, income, race, and ethnicity, or gender, can influence the development of abnormal behaviour.[25]

Multiple causality

The number of different theoretical perspectives in the field of psychological abnormality has made it difficult to properly explain psychopathology. The attempt to explain all mental disorders with the same theory leads to reductionism (explaining a disorder or other complex phenomena using only a single idea or perspective).[26] Most mental disorders are composed of several factors, which is why one must take into account several theoretical perspectives when attempting to diagnose or explain a particular behavioral abnormality or mental disorder. Explaining mental disorders with a combination of theoretical perspectives is known as multiple causality.

The diathesis–stress model emphasizes the importance of applying multiple causality to psychopathology by stressing that disorders are caused by both precipitating causes and predisposing causes. A precipitating cause is an immediate trigger that instigates a person's action or behavior. A predisposing cause is an underlying factor that interacts with the immediate factors to result in a disorder. Both causes play a key role in the development of a psychological disorder. For example, high neuroticism antedates most types of psychopathology.

Recent concepts of abnormality

- *Statistical abnormality* – when a certain behavior/characteristic is relevant to a low percentage of the population. However, this does not necessarily mean that such individuals are suffering from mental illness (for example, statistical abnormalities such as extreme wealth/attractiveness)
- *Psychometric abnormality* – when a certain behavior/characteristic differs from the population's normal dispersion e.g. having an IQ of 35 could be classified as abnormal, as the population average is 100. However, this does not specify a particular mental illness.

- *Deviant behavior* – this is not always a sign of mental illness, as mental illness can occur without deviant behavior, and such behavior may occur in the absence of mental illness.
- *Combinations* – including distress, dysfunction, distorted psychological processes, inappropriate responses in given situations and causing/risking harm to oneself.

Approaches

- *Somatogenic* – abnormality is seen as a result of biological disorders in the brain.[27] This approach has led to the development of radical biological treatments, e.g. lobotomy.
- *Psychogenic* – abnormality is caused by psychological problems. Psychoanalytic (Freud), Cathartic, Hypnotic and Humanistic Psychology (Carl Rogers, Abraham Maslow) treatments were all derived from this paradigm. This approach has, as well, led to some esoteric treatments: Franz Mesmer used to place his patients in a darkened room with music playing, then enter it wearing a flamboyant outfit and poke the "infected" body areas with a stick.

Classification

DSM-5

The standard abnormal psychology and psychiatry reference book in North America is the Diagnostic and Statistical Manual of the American Psychiatric Association. The current version of the book is known as DSM-5. It lists a set of disorders and provides detailed descriptions on what constitutes a disorder such as Major Depressive Disorder or anxiety disorder. It also gives general descriptions of how frequently the disorder occurs in the general population, whether it is more common in males or females and other such facts.

The DSM-5 identifies three key elements that must be present to constitute a mental disorder. These elements include:

- Symptoms that involve disturbances in behavior, thoughts, or emotions.
- Symptoms associated with personal distress or impairment.
- Symptoms that stem from internal dysfunctions (i.e. specifically having biological and/or psychological roots).

The diagnostic process uses five dimensions, each of which is identified as an "axis", to ascertain symptoms and overall functioning of the individual. It is important to note that the DSM-5 no longer uses this axis system. These axes are as follows:

- **Axis I** – *Clinical disorders*, which would include major mental and learning disorders. These disorders make up what is generally acknowledged as a disorder including major depressive disorder, generalized anxiety disorder, schizophrenia, and substance dependence. To be given a diagnosis for a disorder in this axis the patient must meet the criteria for the particular disorder which is presented in the DSM in that particular disorders section. Disorders in this axis are of particular importance because they are likely to have an effect on the individual in many other axes. In fact the first 3 axes are highly related. This axis is similar to what would be considered an illness or disease in general medicine.

- **Axis II** – *Personality Disorders* and a decrease of the use of intellect disorder. This is a very broad axis which contains disorders relating to how the individual functions with the world around him or herself. This axis provides a way of coding for long lasting maladaptive personality characteristics that could have a factor in the expression or development of a disorder on Axis I although this is not always the case. Disorders in this axis include disorders such as antisocial personality disorder, histrionic personality disorder, and paranoid personality disorder. Mental retardation is also coded in this axis although most other learning disabilities are coded in Axis I. This Axis is an example of how the Axes all interact with one another help to give an overall diagnosis for an individual.

- **Axis III** – *General medical conditions* and "Physical disorders". The conditions listed here are the ones that could potentially be relevant to the managing or understanding of the case. Axis III is often used together with an Axis I diagnosis to give a better rounded explanation of the particular disorder. An example of this can be seen in the relationship between major depressive disorder and unremitting pain caused from a chronic medical problem. This category could also include use of drugs and alcohols as these are often symptoms of a disorder themselves such as substance dependence or major depressive disorder. Due to the nature of Axis III it is often recommended that the patient visit a medical doctor when he or she is being assessed in order to determine if the problem could potentially require medical intervention such as surgery. When the first 3 axes are used multiple diagnosis are often found which is actually encouraged by the DSM.

- **Axis IV** – *Psychosocial/environmental problems*, which would contribute to the disorder. Axis IV is used to inspect the broader aspects of a person's situation. This axis will examine the social and environmental factors that could affect the person's diagnosis. Stressors are the main focus of this axis and particular attention is paid to stressors that have been present in the past year; however it is not a requirement that the stressor had to form or continued in the past year. Due to the large number of potential stressors in an individual's life, therapists often find such stressors via a checklist approach which is encouraged by the DSM. An example of the checklist approach would be examine the individual's family life, economic situation, occupation, potential legal problems and so on. It is crucial that the patient is honest in this section as environmental factors can have a huge impact on the patient especially in certain schools of therapy such as the cognitive approach.

- **Axis V** – *Global assessment of functioning (often referred to as GAF)* or "Children's Global Assessment Scale" (for children and teenagers under the age of 18). Axis V is a score given to the patient which is designed to indicate how well the individual is handling their situation at the current time. The GAF is based on a 100-point scale which the examiner will use to give the patient a score. Scores can range from 1 to 100 and depending on the score on the GAF the examiner will decide the best course of action for the patient."According to the manual, scores higher than 70 indicate satisfactory mental health, good overall functioning, and minimal or transient symptoms or impairment, scores between 60 and 70 indicate mild symptoms or impairment, while scores between 50 and 60 indicate moderate symptoms, social or vocational problems, and scores below 50 severe impairment or symptoms". As GAF scores are the final Axis of the DSM the information present in the previous 4 axes are crucial for determining an accurate score.

ICD-10

The major international nosologic system for the classification of mental disorders can be found in the most recent version of the International Classification of Diseases, 10th revision (ICD-10). The ICD-10 has been used by World Health Organization (WHO) Member States since 1994. Chapter five covers some 300 mental and behavioral disorders. The ICD-10's chapter five has been influenced by APA's DSM-IV and there is a great deal of concordance between the two. WHO maintains free access to the ICD-10 Online[28]. Below are the main categories of disorders:

- **F00–F09** Organic, including symptomatic, mental disorders
- **F10–F19** Mental and behavioral disorders due to psychoactive substance use
- **F20–F29** Schizophrenia, schizotypal and delusional disorders
- **F30–F39** Mood [affective] disorders
- **F40–F48** Neurotic, stress-related and somatoform disorders
- **F50–F59** Behavioral syndromes associated with physiological disturbances and physical factors
- **F60–F69** Disorders of adult personality and behavior

- **F70–F79** Mental retardation
- **F80–F89** Disorders of psychological development
- **F90–F98** Behavioral and emotional disorders with onset usually occurring in childhood and adolescence
- **F99** Unspecified mental disorder

Perspectives of Abnormal psychology

Psychologists may use different perspectives to try to get better understanding on abnormal psychology. Some of them may just concentrate on a single perspective. But the professionals prefer to combine two or three perspectives together in order to get significant information for better treatments.

- Behavioral- the perspective focus on observable behaviors
- Medical- the perspective focus on biological causes on mental illness
- Cognitive- the perspective focus on how internal thoughts, perceptions and reasoning contribute to psychological disorders

Cause

Genetics

- Investigated through family studies, mainly of monozygotic (identical) and dizygotic (fraternal) twins, often in the context of adoption. Monozygotic twins should be more likely than dizygotic twins to have the same disorder because they share 100% of their genetic material, whereas dizygotic twins share only 50%. For many disorders, this is exactly what research shows. But given that monozygotic twins share 100% of their genetic material, it may be expected of them to have the same disorders 100% of the time, but in fact they have the same disorders only about 50% of the time[29]
- These studies allow calculation of a *heritability coefficient.*

Biological causal factors

- Neurotransmitter [imbalances of neurotransmitters like norepinephrine, dopamine, serotonin and GABA (Gamma aminobutryic acid)] and hormonal imbalances in the brainWikipedia:Citation needed
- Genetic vulnerabilities
- Constitutional liabilities [physical handicaps and temperament]
- Brain dysfunction and neural plasticity
- Physical deprivation or disruption [deprivation of basic physiological needs]

Socio-cultural factors

- Effects of urban/rural dwelling, gender and minority status on state of mind
- Generalizations about cultural practices and beliefs may fail to capture the diversity that exists within and across cultural groups, so we must be extremely careful not to stereotype individuals of any cultural group

Systemic factors

- Family systems
- Negatively Expressed Emotion playing a part in schizophrenic relapse and anorexia nervosa.

Biopsychosocial factors

- Illness dependent on stress "triggers".

Therapies

Psychoanalysis (Freud)

Psychoanalytic theory is heavily based on the theory of the neurologist Sigmund Freud. These ideas often represented repressed emotions and memories from a patient's childhood. According to psychoanalytic theory, these repressions cause the disturbances that people experience in their daily lives and by finding the source of these disturbances, one should be able to eliminate the disturbance itself. This is accomplished by a variety of methods, with some popular ones being free association, hypnosis, and insight. The goal of these methods is to induce a catharsis or emotional release in the patient which should indicate that the source of the problem has been tapped and it can then be helped. Freud's psychosexual stages also played a key role in this form of therapy; as he would often believe that problems the patient was experiencing were due to them becoming stuck or "fixated" in a particular stage. Dreams also played a major role in this form of therapy as Freud viewed dreams as a way to gain insight into the unconscious mind. Patients were often asked to keep dream journals and to record their dreams to bring in for discussion during the next therapy session. There are many potential problems associated with this style of therapy, including resistance to the repressed memory or feeling, and negative transference onto the therapist. Psychoanalysis was carried on by many after Freud including his daughter Ana Freud and Jacques Lacan. These and many others have gone on to elaborate on Freud's original theory and to add their own take on defense mechanisms or dream analysis. While psychoanalysis has fallen out of favor to more modern forms of therapy it is still used by some clinical psychologists to varying degrees.

Behavioral therapy (Wolpe)

Behavior therapy relies on the principles of behaviorism, such as involving classical and operant conditioning. Behaviorism arose in the early 20th century due to the work of psychologists such as James Watson and B. F. Skinner. Behaviorism states that all behaviors humans do is because of a stimulus and reinforcement. While this reinforcement is normally for good behavior, it can also occur for maladaptive behavior. In this therapeutic view, the patients maladaptive behavior has been reinforced which will cause the maladaptive behavior to be repeated. The goal of the therapy is to reinforce less maladaptive behaviors so that with time these adaptive behaviors will become the primary ones in the patient.

Humanistic therapy (Rogers)

Humanistic therapy aims to achieve self-actualization (Carl Rogers, 1961). In this style of therapy, the therapist will focus on the patient themselves as opposed to the problem which the patient is afflicted with. The overall goal of this therapy is that by treating the patient as "human" instead of client will help get to the source of the problem and hopefully resolve the problem in an effective manner. Humanistic therapy has been on the rise in recent years and has been associated with numerous positive benefits. It is considered to be one of the core elements needed therapeutic effectiveness and a significant contributor to not only the well being of the patient but society as a whole. Some say that all of the therapeutic approaches today draw from the humanistic approach in some regard and that humanistic therapy is the best way for treat a patient. Humanistic therapy can be used on people of all ages; however, it is very popular among children in its variant known as "play therapy". Children are often sent to therapy due to outburst that they have in a school or home setting, the theory is that by treating the child in a setting that is similar to the area that they are having their disruptive behavior, the child will be more likely to learn from the therapy and have an effective outcome. In play therapy, the clinicians will "play" with their client usually with toys, or a tea party. Playing is the typical behavior of a child and therefore playing with the therapist will come as a natural response to the child. In playing together the clinician will ask the patient questions but due to the setting; the questions no longer seem intrusive and therapeutic more like a normal conversation. This should help the patient realizes issues they have and confess them to the therapist with less difficulty than they may experience in a traditional counselling setting.

Cognitive behavioural therapy (Ellis and Beck)

Cognitive behavioural therapy aims to influence thought and cognition (Beck, 1977). This form of therapy relies on not only the components of behavioral therapy as mentioned before, but also the elements of cognitive psychology.

This relies on not only the clients behavioral problems that could have arisen from conditioning; but also there negative schemas, and distorted perceptions of the world around them. These negative schemas may be causing distress in the life of the patient; for example the schemas may be giving them unrealistic expectations for how well they should perform at their job, or how they should look physically. When these expectations are not met it will often result in maladaptive behaviors such as depression, obsessive compulsions, and anxiety. With cognitive behavior therapy; the goal is to change the schemas that are causing the stress in a persons life and hopefully replace them with more realistic ones. Once the negative schemas have been replaced, it will hopefully cause a remission of the patients symptoms. CBT is considered particularly effective in the treatment of depression and has even been used lately in group settings. It is felt that using CBT in a group setting aids in giving its members a sense of support and decreasing the likelihood of them dropping out of therapy before the treatment has had time to work properly. CBT has been found to be an effective treatments for many patients even those who do not have diseases and disorders typically thought of as psychiatric ones. For example, patients with the disease multiple sclerosis have found a lot of help using CBT. The treatment often helps the patients cope with the disorder they have and how they can adapt to their new lives without developing new problems such as depression or negative schemas about themselves.

According to RAND, therapies are difficult to provide to all patients in need. A lack of funding and understanding of symptoms provides a major roadblock that is not easily avoided. Individual symptoms and responses to treatments vary, creating a disconnect between patient, society and care givers/professionals.

References

- Bennett, Paul (2003). "Abnormal and Clinical Psychology". Open University Press. ISBN 978-0-335-21236-1.<templatestyles src="Module:Citation/CS1/styles.css"></templatestyles>
- Hansell, James; Lisa Damour (2005). *Abnormal Psychology*. Von Hoffman Press. ISBN 0-471-38982-X.<templatestyles src="Module:Citation/CS1/styles.css"></templatestyles>
- Barlow, David H.; Vincent Mark Durand (2004). *Abnormal Psychology: An Integrative Approach*. Thomson Wadsworth. ISBN 0-534-63362-5.<templatestyles src="Module:Citation/CS1/styles.css"></templatestyles>
- Cherry, Kendra (May 9, 2016). "What Is Abnormal Psychology?"[30]. *Verywell*. Retrieved 2017-03-10.<templatestyles src="Module:Citation/CS1/styles.css"></templatestyles>

- Ormel, J.; Jeronimus, B.F.; Kotov, R.; Riese, H.; Bos, E.H.; Hankin, B. (2013). "Neuroticism and common mental disorders: Meaning and utility of a complex relationship"[31]. *Clinical Psychology Review*. **33** (5): 686–697. doi: 10.1016/j.cpr.2013.04.003[32]. PMC 4382368[31]. PMID 23702592[33].<templatestyles src="Module:Citation/CS1/styles.css"></templatestyles>

External links

> Library resources about
> **Abnormal psychology**
>
> - Resources in your library[34]
> - Resources in other libraries[35]

- Abnormal Psychology Students Practice Resources[36]
- Zvolensky, M. J.; Kotov, R.; Antipova, A. V.; Schmidt, N. B. (2005). "Diathesis stress model for panic-related distress: A test in a Russian epidemiological sample". *Behaviour Research and Therapy*. **43** (4): 521–532. doi: 10.1016/j.brat.2004.09.001[37]. PMID 15701361[38].<templatestyles src="Module:Citation/CS1/styles.css"></templatestyles>
- Psychology Terms[39]
- Psychology Terms – a 600-page dictionary pdf[40]
- A Course in Abnormal Psychology[41]

Further reading

Understanding behavior makes it more normal[42]

Why Young Patients with Cancer Require Different Coping Tools?[43]

EEG Correlation during Social Decision-making in Institutionalized Adolescents[44]

Appendix

References

[1] Miller, A. C. (2006). Jundi-Shapur, bimaristans, and the rise of academic medical centres. Journal of the Royal Society of Medicine, 99(12), 615–617. doi:10.1258/jrsm.99.12.615

[2] Youssef, H. A., Youssef, F. A., & Dening, T. R. (1996). Evidence for the existence of schizophrenia in medieval Islamic society. History of Psychiatry, 7(25), 055–62. doi:10.1177/0957154x9600702503

[3] Torrey comments that very early mental illness descriptions do not seem to fit schizophrenia, there is a 'sporadic presence' from the 17th century, and then c. 1800 "suddenly... it appeared."

[4] |url=https://online.csp.edu/blog/psychology/history-of-mental-illness-treatment |journal= Hussung, Tricia "A History of Mental Illness Treatment: Obsolete Practices" |

[5] https://books.google.com/books?id=nfvaX3eyYjEC

[6] //www.worldcat.org/oclc/54460256

[7] https://books.google.com/books?id=wzlJWvCoNKQC

[8] //www.worldcat.org/oclc/50253057

[9] http://ark.cdlib.org/ark:/13030/ft9r29p2x5/

[10] //www.worldcat.org/oclc/17982761

[11] //www.worldcat.org/oclc/45404661

[12] //www.worldcat.org/oclc/818987861

[13] https://books.google.com/books?id=g3naAAAAMAAJ

[14] //en.wikipedia.org/w/index.php?title=Template:Psychology_sidebar&action=edit

[15] Abnormal psychology http://assets.pearsonglobalschools.com/asset_mgr/current/201214/PsychologyChapter5.pdf

[16] James Hansell and Lisa Damour. *Abnormal Psychology*. Ch 3. pp. 30–33.

[17] Nolen-Hoeksema, Susan (2013). *Abnormal Psychology* (6th ed.). Boston: McGraw-Hill.

[18] Rimm, David C., and John W. Somervill. Abnormal Psychology. New York: Academic, 1977. Print.

[19] Nolen-Hoeksema, Susan (2013). Abnormal Psychology (6th ed.). Boston: McGraw-Hill.

[20] Jones, Billy E. Treating the Homeless: Urban Psychiatry's Challenge. Washington, D.C.: American Psychiatric, 1986. Print.

[21] David H. Barlow and Vincent Mark Durand (2004). *Abnormal Psychology: An Integrative Approach*. p. 7

[22] David H. Barlow and Vincent Mark Durand (2004). *Abnormal Psychology: An Integrative Approach*. p. 8

[23] David H. Barlow and Vincent Mark Durand (2004). *Abnormal Psychology: An Integrative Approach*. p. 11

[24] David H. Barlow and Vincent Mark Durand (2004). *Abnormal Psychology: An Integrative Approach*. p. 26

[25] Richard P. Halgin

[26] James Hansell and Lisa Damour. *Abnormal Psychology*. Ch 3. p. 37.

[27] Kraeplin, 1883

[28] http://www.who.int/classifications/icd/en/

[29] http://www.blackwellpublishing.com/intropsych/pdf/chapter15.pdf

[30] https://www.verywell.com/what-is-abnormal-psychology-2794775

[31] //www.ncbi.nlm.nih.gov/pmc/articles/PMC4382368

[32] //doi.org/10.1016%2Fj.cpr.2013.04.003

[33] //www.ncbi.nlm.nih.gov/pubmed/23702592

[34] //tools.wmflabs.org/ftl/cgi-bin/ftl?st=wp&su=abnormal+psychology

[35] //tools.wmflabs.org/ftl/cgi-bin/ftl?st=wp&su=abnormal+psychology&library=0CHOOSE0

[36] https://web.archive.org/web/20080108152418/http://minnay.com/products/

[37] //doi.org/10.1016%2Fj.brat.2004.09.001

[38] //www.ncbi.nlm.nih.gov/pubmed/15701361

[39] http://dictionary-psychology.com

[40] https://web.archive.org/web/20170712233214/http://english4success.ru/Upload/books/1278.pdf

[41] https://web.archive.org/web/20091202022810/http://ccvillage.buffalo.edu/Abpsy/

[42] https://ahnthinkinglab.yale.edu/sites/default/files/files/Papers/ahnnovickkim2003-1.pdf

[43] https://www.omicsonline.org/open-access/why-young-patients-with-cancer-require-different-coping-tools-2472-0496-1000129.pdf

[44] https://www.omicsonline.org/open-access/eeg-correlation-during-social-decisionmaking-in-institutionalizedadolescents-2472-0496-1000131.pdf

Article Sources and Contributors

The sources listed for each article provide more detailed licensing information including the copyright status, the copyright owner, and the license conditions.

History of mental disorders *Source:* https://en.wikipedia.org/w/index.php?oldid=862840703 *License:* Creative Commons Attribution-Share Alike 3.0 *Contributors:*   116181ep, Aadhyaa Udawat, Adavidb, Aitias, Amillar, Ariel., Aumtof6, BD2412, Billinghurst, Bruhhhh2021, CV9933, Cann0torcani, Casliber, Chris the speller, Citation bot 1, Classicwiki, ClueBot NG, DR04, Darkish Raven, Darrencdm1988, Davehi1, Dawnseeker2000, Dialectric, Diptanshu Das, Discospinster, Dragoon17, Emesee, EverSince, Evrik, Fayedizard, Fdskjs, FiachraByrne, Fibo1123581321, Flyer22 Reborn, Footwarrior, Forgottenfaces, Fratrep, Gaius Cornelius, Geb11, Grafen, Guy1890, HarlandQPitt, Headbomb, Hmains, Humorideas, I dream of horses, Ingolfson, Iridescent, J.delanoy, J04n, JCJC777, Jagged 85, Jcbutler, John of Reading, Johnfos, Jojalozzo, Jonesey95, Jrun, Julesd, Julienre, KATANAGOD, KConWiki, Katolophyromai, Klbrain, LilHelpa, Lova Falk, MathewTownsend, MelbourneStar, MikeLynch, Mirokado, Mu301, MusikAnimal, NickPenguin, Nondropframe, NottNott, Ohconfucius, Ombudsman, Orphan Wiki, Ospalh, P64, Pdcook, PhnomPencil, Pinethicket, R'n'B, Rathfelder, Riceissa, Rich Farmbrough, Rjwilmsi, S. M. Sullivan, SchreiberBike, ScottyBerg, Shangrilalala711, Shaun, ShelleyAdams, Shellwood, Shoveling Ferret, Singinglemon~enwiki, Skittleys, Standardname, Stevegallery, Storm Rider, Surv1v4l1st, Syncategoremata, The Anome, Thirdright, Tiberius Aug, Tide rolls, Tjankows, Tmgonzalez, Topbanana, Trappist the monk, Trugster, Vero.Verite, Wahwahpedal, Wavelength, Widr, William Avery, Wingspeed, Wotnow, WriterHound, Yunshui, 118 anonymous edits 1

Abnormal psychology *Source:* https://en.wikipedia.org/w/index.php?oldid=862579073 *License:* Creative Commons Attribution-Share Alike 3.0 *Contributors:*   Aaron Kauppi, Ajeelani, Alexkvaskov, AliceYangSun, Anachronist, Arjayay, ArtemisDSII, BD2412, Bender235, Bgiro1, Bioguodong, Boleyn, Buffbills7701, Burningview, Byzantophile, Cerabot~enwiki, Chris Capoccia, Citation bot 1, ClueBot NG, Cosmic Latte, Crystal.shi, Davidshq, Dewritech, Dgthomas07, Doc James, Donner60, DoveMustard11456, DrKay, EagerToddler39, Eddy7748, Encladeus, Excirial, Falcon8765, Fbarw, FiachraByrne, Flyer22 Reborn, Fredlox87, Fæ, Gaia Octavia Agrippa, Gary, Gazelle55, Gemmabell, Gham1990, Gilliam, Gmli82164, HeartofGod, Hiersgarr, Hmvaid, Iridescent, Iss246, JHewitt88, Ja172984, Jackscullin1, Jackywsj, Jacobisq, Jajhill, Jarble, Jcbutler, Jeevankumarkode, Jenever Spirit, Jengirl1988, Jeraphine Gryphon, Jhertel, Jialuzeng, Jlucas1, John of Reading, Judicatus, Julietdeltalima, Jusdafax, Kagundu, Kuru, KylieTastic, Lidaijin, Lissamg, LittleWink, Lizia7, Lova Falk, Mandarax, Manveer.grewal, Mark Ironie, Markwarnes, Masterpiece2000, Materialscientist, Mayrapm128, McGeddon, Mcps39, Me, Myself, and I are Here, Mesabird, Metrowestjp, Mild Bill Hiccup, Moyin G, Mr magic straw, MrScorch6200, MsTumnus101, MusikAnimal, Nehadokania08, NeonHD, Neutrality, Nihiltres, ONEder Boy, Oluwa2Chainz, Ongmianli, Oshwah, Paine Ellsworth, Penbat, Petrb, Pietrow, Psya01hwiki, Pwatson5291, R'n'B, Reaper Eternal, Remember, RhubarbX3, Rjwilmsi, RobinHood70, Sagana2093, Sanya3, Sct72, Shellwood, Shumdw, Skarebo, Slungup, Sndenny1234, SnowBooker, Stesmo, Steve carlson, SuperHamster, TAnthony, THEN WHO WAS PHONE?, TJ Diluvio, Tbhotch, Teddy.william, The Thing That Should Not Be, The Transhumanist, Theopolisme, Tomar2428, Tomwood0, Trillium.moss, Trilobitealive, Trinity507, Tweak279, Umama.Ahmed, WMakkers, WereSpielChequers, Widr, WikiHead, Xndr, Xuke19891225, Xushuo2, Yazmindeebayram, Zhangm28, Zhyr, Лев Дубовой, 154 anonymous edits 13

Image Sources, Licenses and Contributors

The sources listed for each image provide more detailed licensing information including the copyright status, the copyright owner, and the license conditions.

Image *Source:* https://en.wikipedia.org/w/index.php?title=File:Lock-green.svg *License:* Creative Commons Zero *Contributors:* User:Trappist the monk 12
Image *Source:* https://en.wikipedia.org/w/index.php?title=File:Psi2.svg *License:* Public Domain *Contributors:* User:Gdh~commonswiki 13

License

Index